かみ彫刻

谷内庸生

PAPER SCULPTURE 2

tsuneo taniuchi

pieces of the universe

はじめに

紙と話が出来ない時、
私は良く散歩に出かけます。
夜空は私の想像力をかきたててくれます。
　夜空を切り裂く流れ星。
　時が流れ、一つ一つの星に名前ができ、
　物語が始まる。
　道化師はいそいそと町に出、
　酒をつがれ、踊りが始まる。
　暗い茶室に月がともり、
　老人が現われる。
　宇宙の会話がかわされ、
　道化師たちが耳をかたむける。
　老人は言う。
　宇宙はあなたの中にあるよと。
こんないかにも個人的な空間を、
紙に表現してみたかったのです。
今回、掲載した作品は前回の「かみ彫刻」の星を発展させ、
宇宙をテーマに表現したものです。紙を切り、折り曲げながら
あなた自身の宇宙を楽しんでください。

Foreword

When I can't very well converse with paper I often go out
for a walk, for the night sky stimulates my imagination
more than anything else does.
　I see a shooting star tear away and vanish.
　But thousands and millions of other stars remain.
　Time passes by.
　Each star comes to get its own name.
　And stories are made and told.
　Now I see pierrots go to town,
　light in heart and in steps.
　Wine is poured. Dance begins.
　There's a dark tea-room.
　The moon is lit inside.
　An old man appears. He talks about the universe.
　Pierrots listen...
　The old man ends his talk, saying
　"You see now that the universe is right in your heart".
So, I decided to make "universe" the theme of my works
in "Paper Sculpture 2", to satisfy my desire to express the
very private of my thoughts. I hope you also enjoy your
own conception of the universe while cutting and folding
paper.

「かゞみ彫刻・宇宙」の魅力
Paper Sculpture pieces of the universe

●著者略歴　1953年―和歌山県生まれ　1975年―日本大学芸術学部卒業　1975～77年―デザイン会社勤務　1978年―渡米　1979年～82年―ボストンの教育テレビ局WGBH，W.F.E.M建築事務所に勤務　1982年―ボストンにスタジオを設立。ニューヨーク近代美術館，ボストン美術館，ハーバード大学などをクライアントとし，編集デザイン，ポスター，ロゴタイプ，カードデザインなどで活躍　1985年11月―草月会館にて個展開催　1985年12月―「アルファベット・ランデブー」インスタレーション開催　●主な受賞歴　1980年―TDC銅賞　1982・83年―ニューイングランド・ブックショー・デザイン賞　1983年―ボストン，ニューヨークADC編集部門賞　●作品集　1983年―「アルファベット・ランデブー」を自費出版　1985年―「かゞみ彫刻」玄光社刊

●**Author's Biographical Sketch** 1953－Born in Wakayama Prefecture, Japan. 1975－Graduated from Japan University College of Art. 1978－Moved to the United States. 1979～82－Employed by WGBH, Boston Educational Television Foundation. W.F.E.M. Architect office. 1982－Established Taniuchi Design Studio. Projects include editorial design, posters, logotypes, and greeting cards for various clients including the New York Museum of Moderm Art, Boston Museum of Fine Arts, and Harvard University. November 1985－Opens one-man show at Tokyo's Sogetsu Kaikan. December 1985 －installation of Alphabet Rendezvous by the seaside of Tanabe. ●**Major Professional Awards and Activities** 1980－Type Directors Club Awards for Typographic Excellence　1982, 83－New England Book Show Design Awards　1983－Boston and New York Art Director's Club Award for Editorial Design ●**Books published** 1983－"Alphabet Rendezvous" Private publication 1985－"Paper Sculpture" published by Genko-sha

●谷内庸生作品集「かゞみ彫刻・2　断片的宇宙」　●発行・編集人―北原守夫　●編集―企画編集室・原由樹夫　●アートディレクション＆デザイン―谷内庸生　●写真―伏見行介＋室沢敏晴　●詩＋翻訳―石田達夫　●発行所―株式会社玄光社　東京都千代田区飯田橋4-1-5　〒102　電話03（263）3511㈹　振替番号・東京7―17063　●印刷―三浦印刷株式会社　©昭和62年6月1日発行　●定価1,500円

●**Collected Works of Tsuneo Taniuchi**－Paper Sculpture 2 pieces of the universe ●**Publication and Editing**－Morio Kitahara ●**Coordinating Editor**－Yukio Hara ●**Art Direction and Design**－Tsuneo Taniuchi ●**Photography**－Yukisuke Fushimi＋Toshiharu Murosawa ●**Poetic Titles and Translation**－Tatsuo Ishida ●**Publisher**－Genko-sha Co., Ltd. Iidabashi 4-1-5,Chiyoda-ku, Tokyo-to 102, Japan. Telephone: 03-263-3511 ●**Printing**－Miura Printing Co., Ltd. ●**Copyright and Publication Date**－ June 1987

ISBN4-7683-0003-0

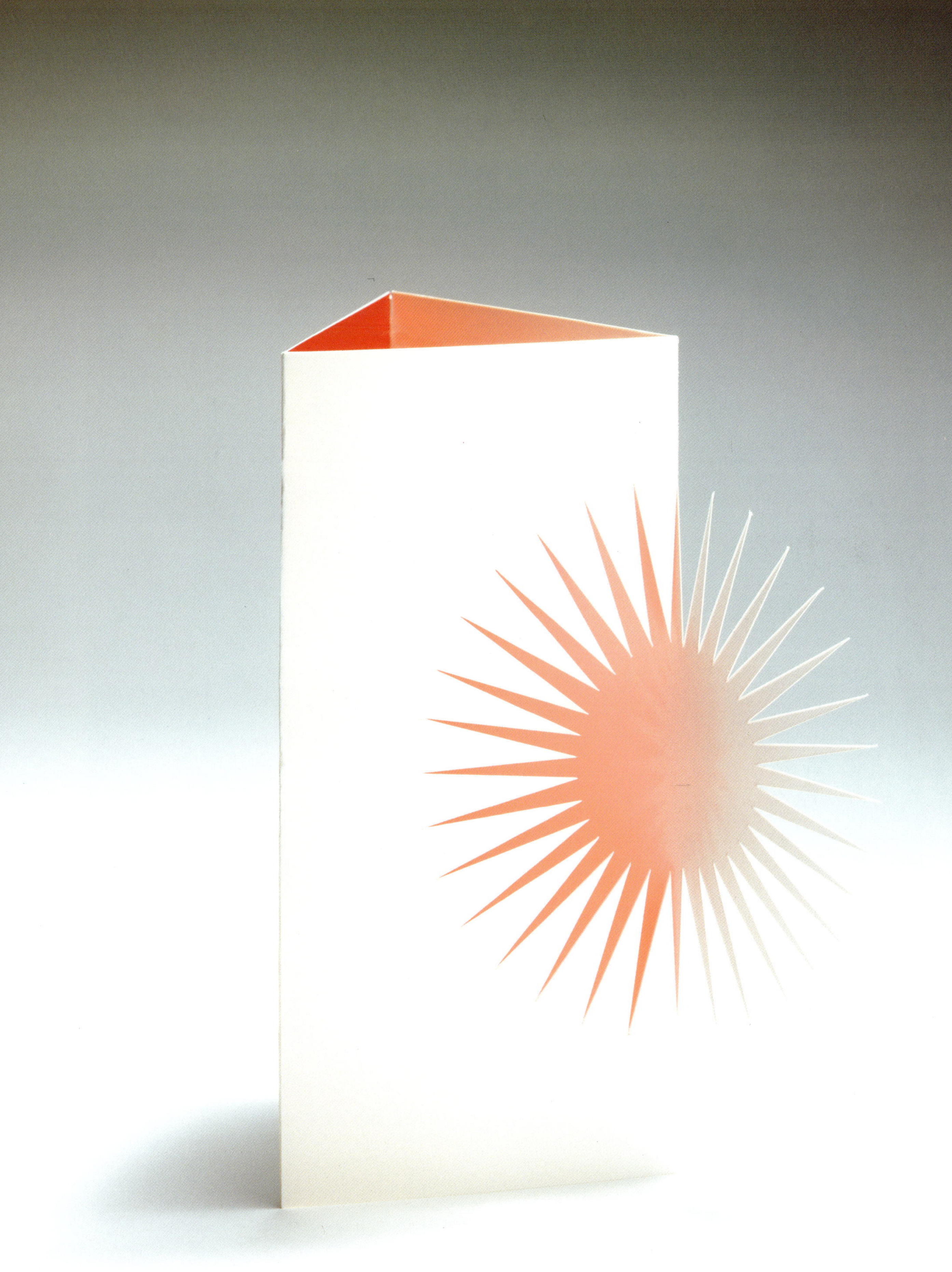

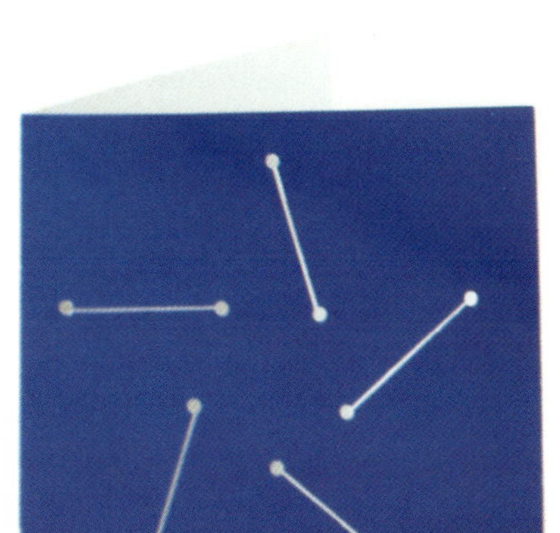
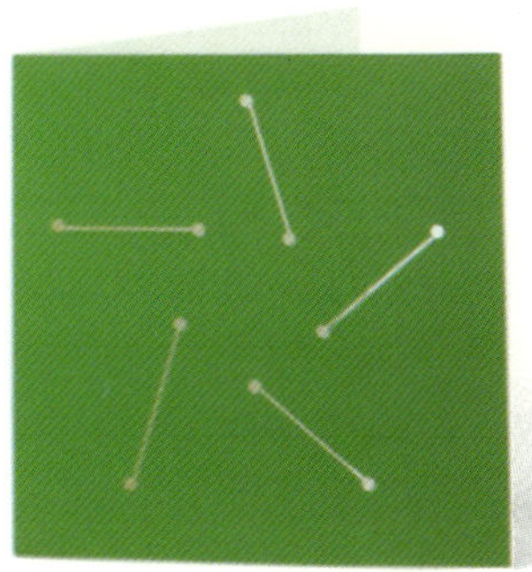

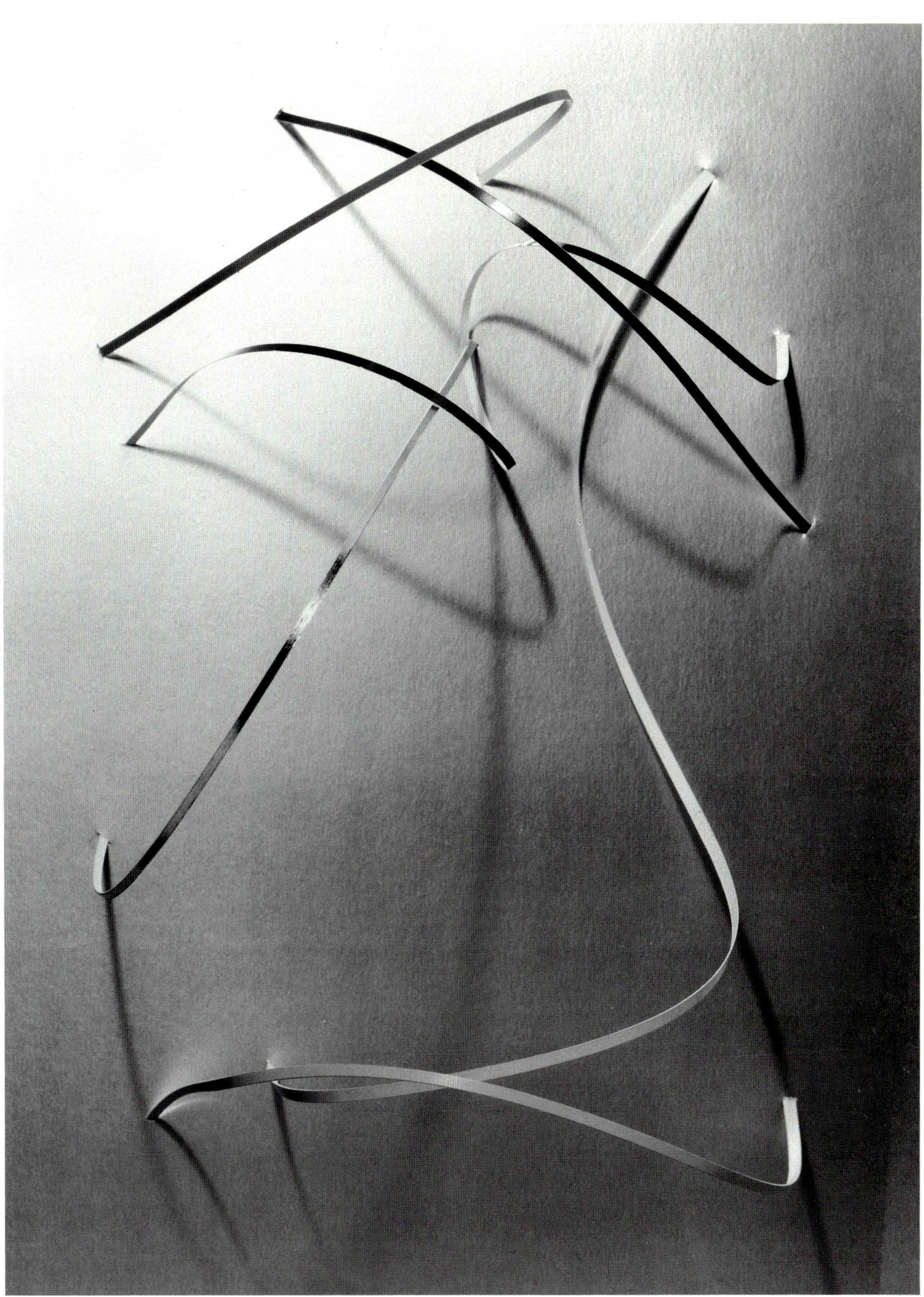

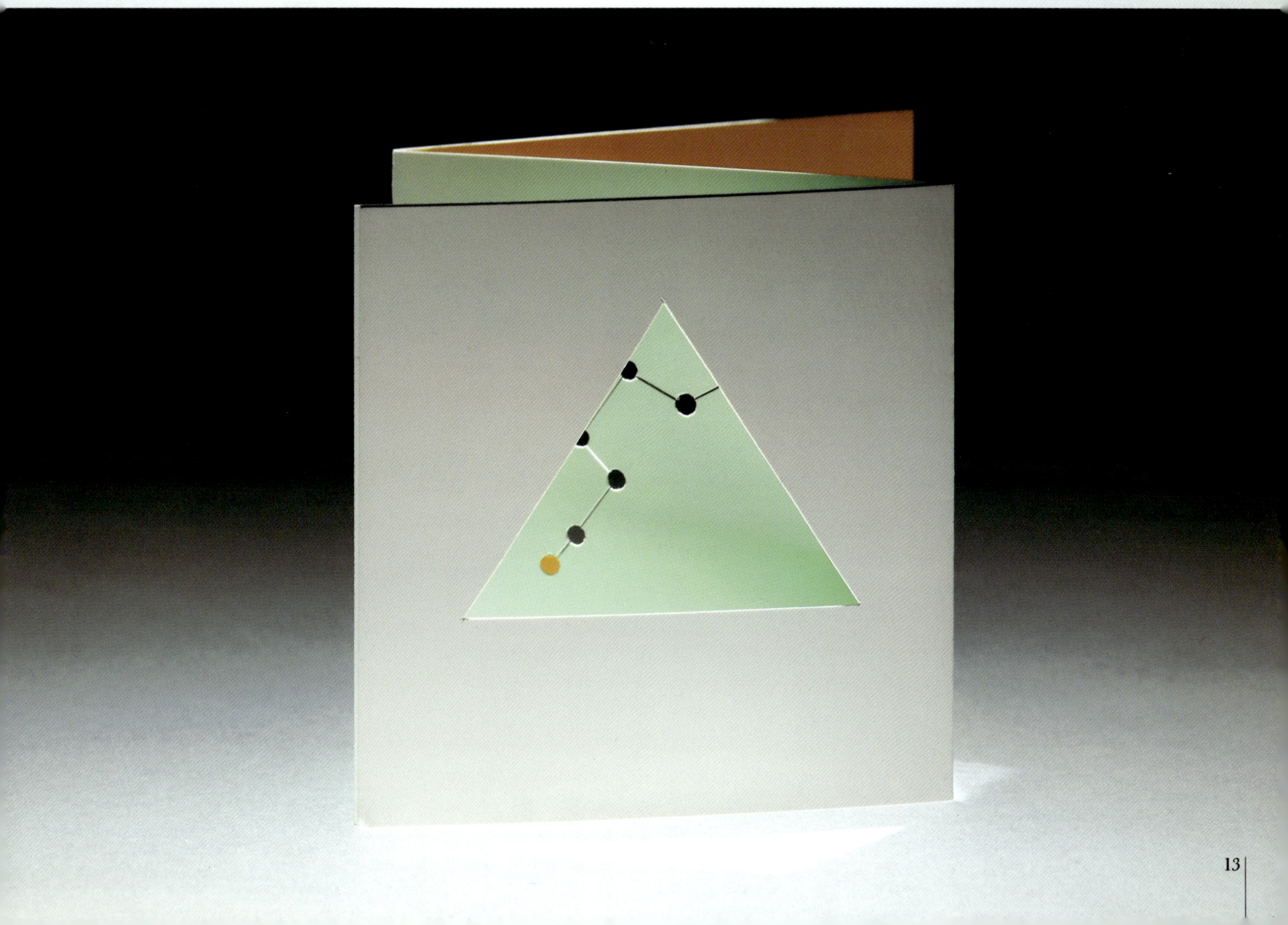

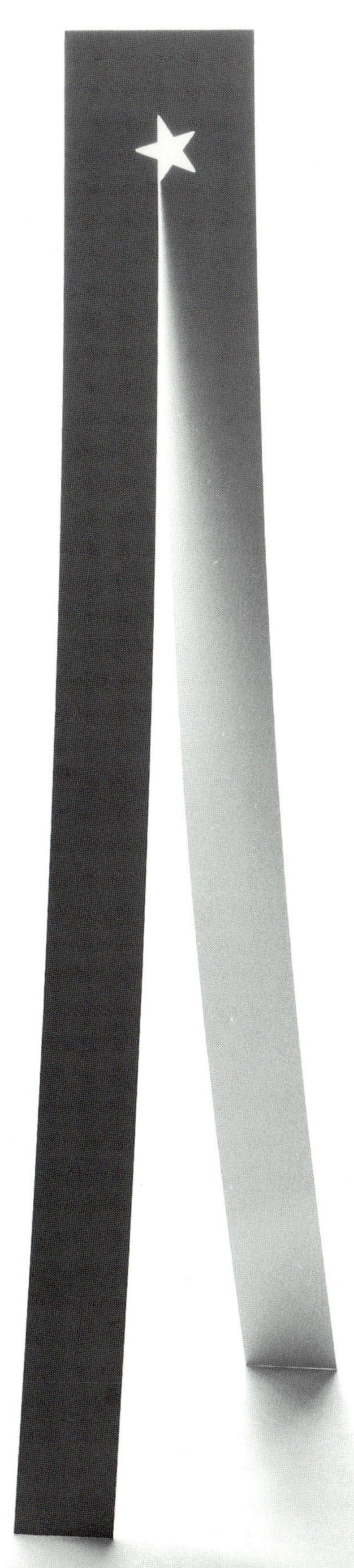

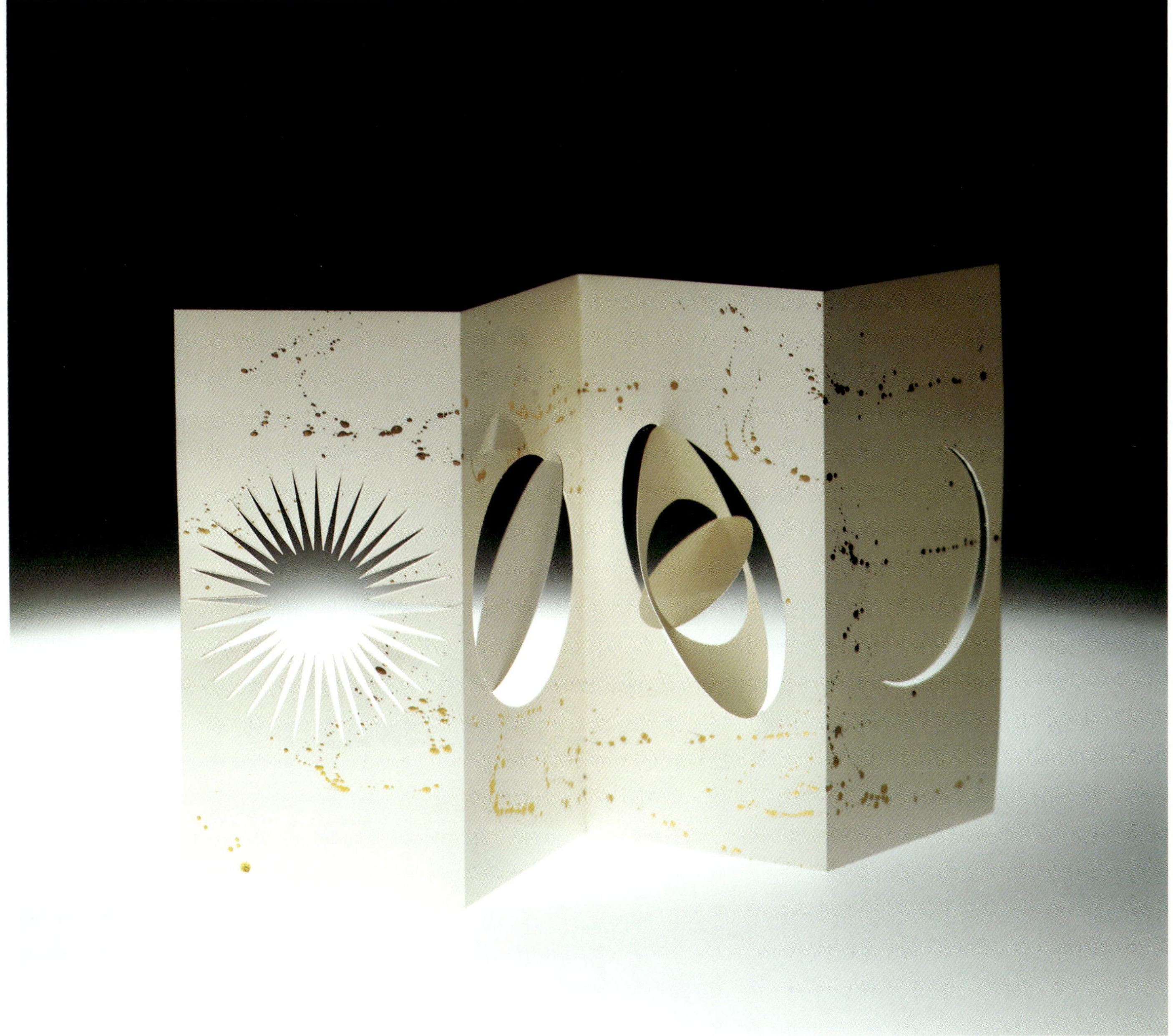

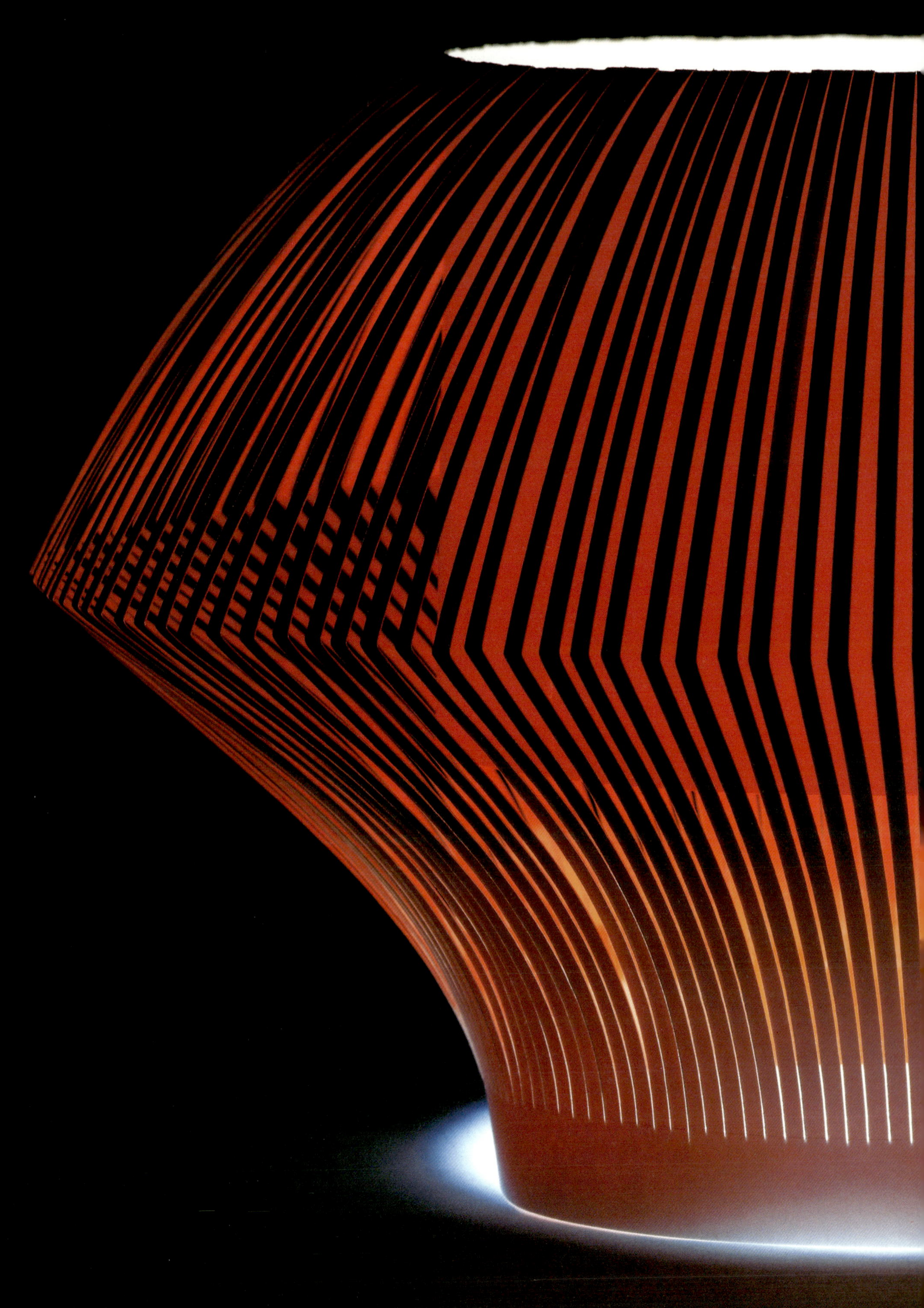

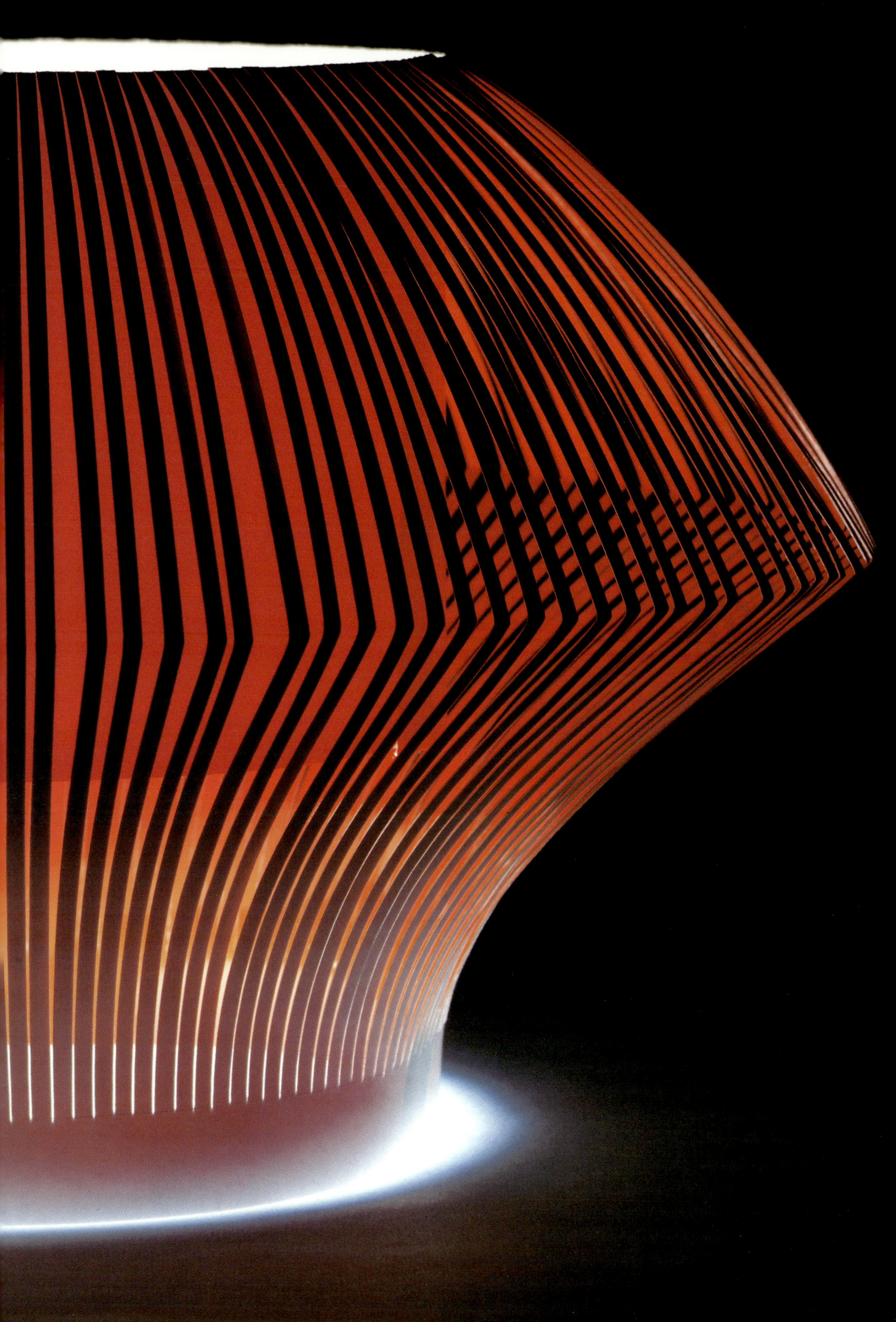

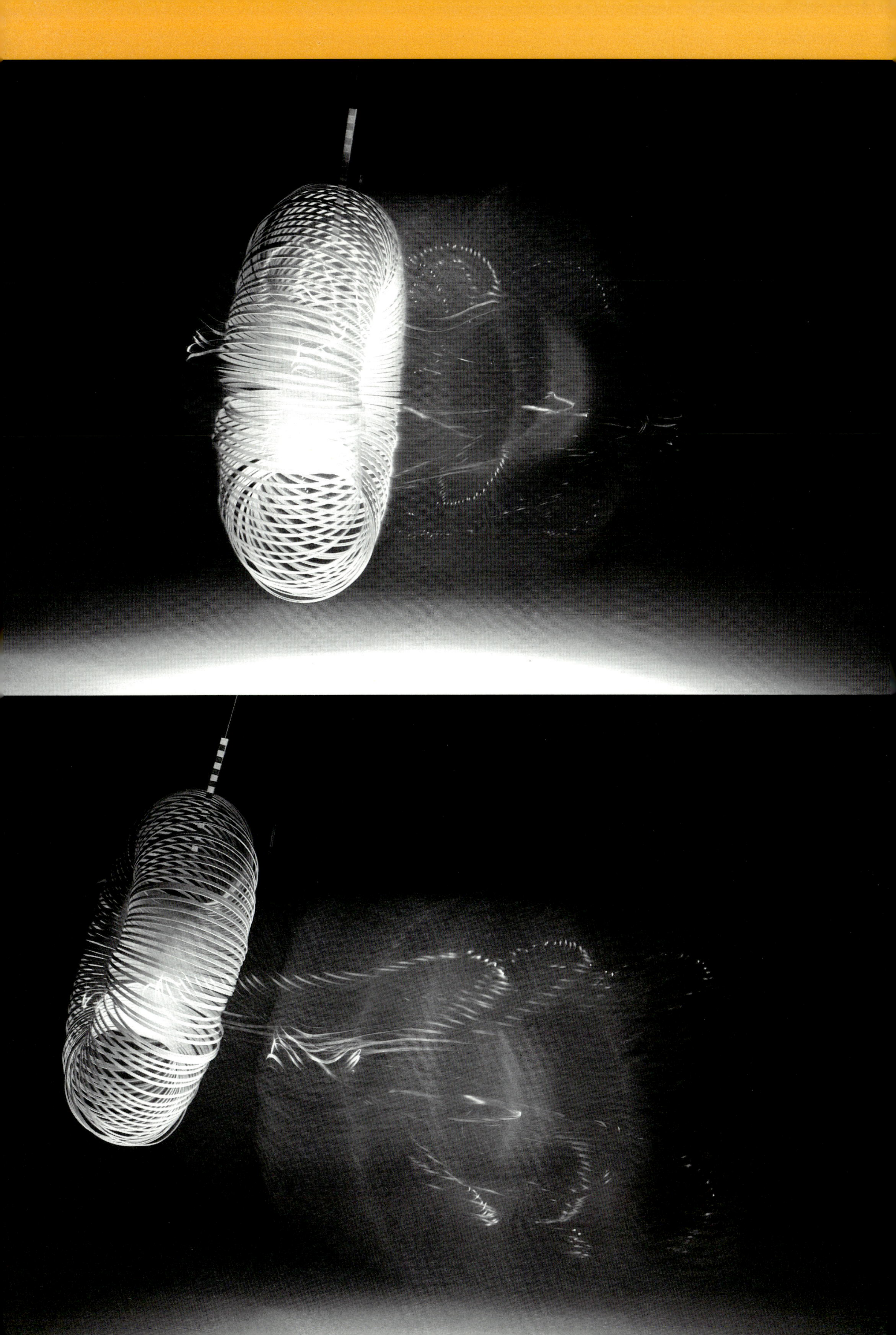

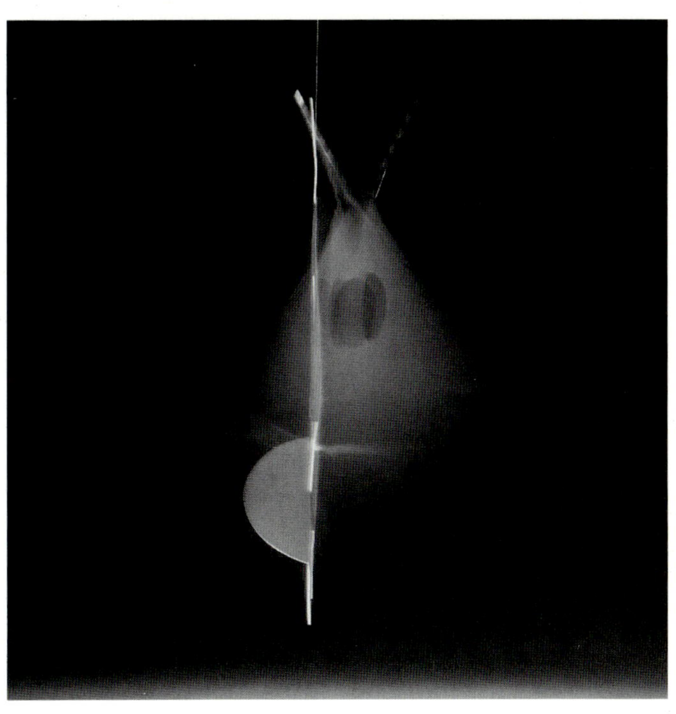 

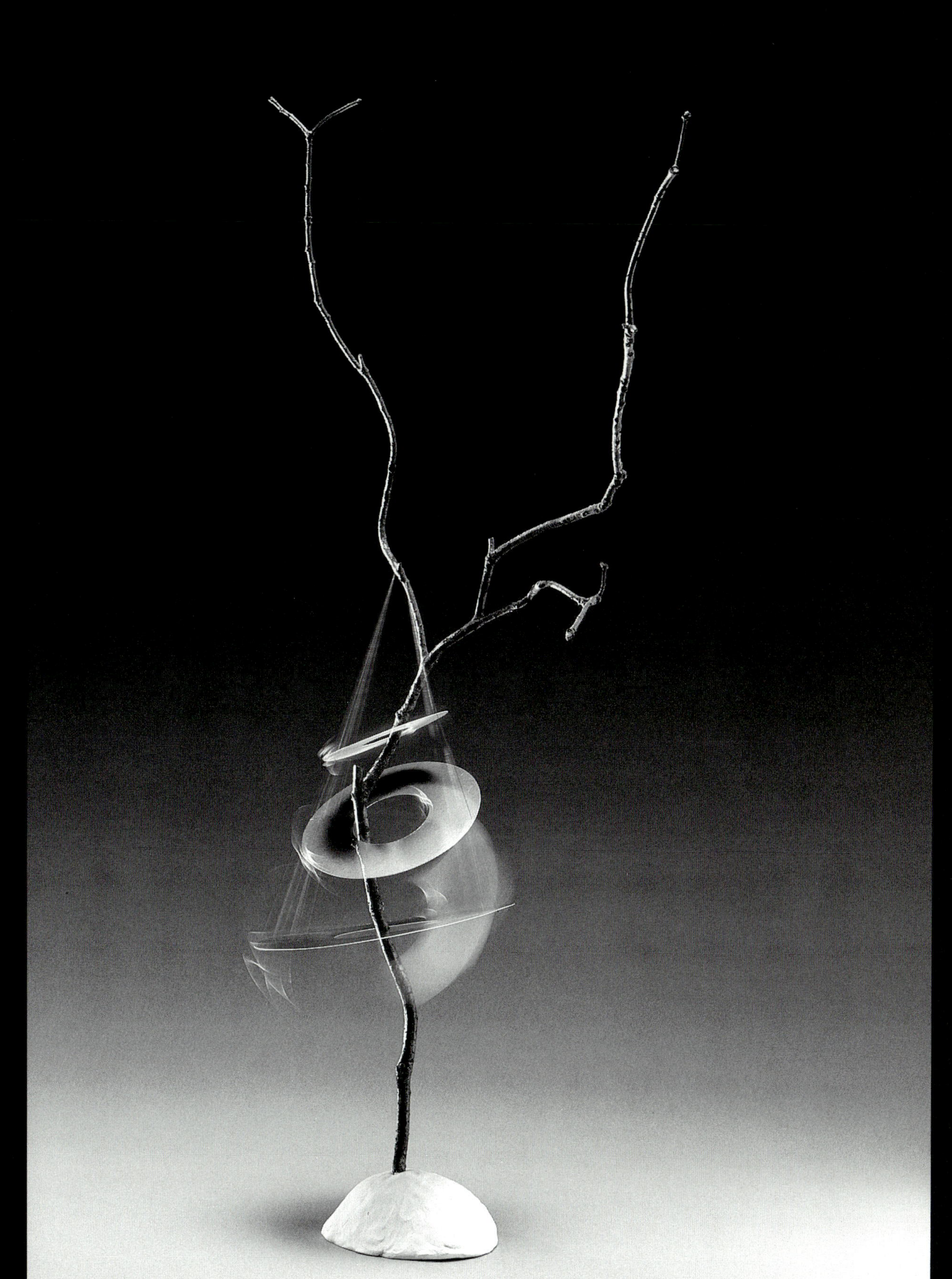

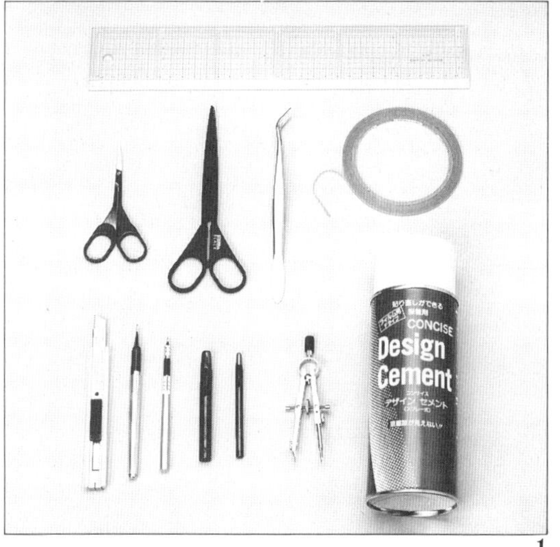

作り方

「かみ彫刻」はカッター1本で作ることができますが、きれいに作るには少し道具を用意してください（写真1）。カッターは2種類、直線を切る先の鋭いものと曲線を切る丸刃のものがあると便利です。定規はスチール製のものかプラスチック製のものを使います（写真2）。穴はパンチであけます（写真3）。色紙も必要です。作品2などのリフレクションを楽しむ作品に使います（写真4）。接着剤も普通のもののほかに両面テープなどを用意して置くと便利です。作品6、18、表紙、25の作り方は写真5、6、7、8を参考にしてください。

How to Construct Paper Sculpture

Although one can make these paper sculptures using nothing more than a regular mat knife, a few other tools are useful for maximum precision (photo 1). Two types of mat knives come in handy, a regular one with a sharp blade for cutting straight lines, and one with a circular blade for cutting curves. Use a plastic or steel ruler (photo 2). For making holes use a paper punch (photo 3). You will also need some colored paper as used in Piece 2 (photo 4). For adhering prepare two sided tape as well as regular one sided tape.

If you want to try Pieces 6,18, the work on the cover and 25, photos 5, 6, 7 and 8 will be useful.

型紙の中の記号は

―― 切り取り線
Cut along this line

‥‥‥ 折 り 線
Fold along this line

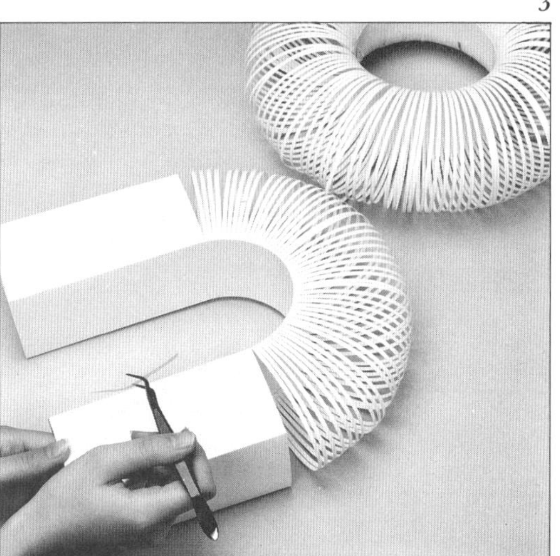

型紙 1

この頁から48頁にかけて収載した
作品10点（作品番号 6、7、11、13、
17、18、19、20、25、26）の型紙
は、この型紙をトレースし「かみ
彫刻」を作るものです。

Pattern 1

The patterns of 10 works
(Piece Nos. 6, 7, 11, 13, 17, 18,
19, 20, 25 and 26) printed on
the pages (from this page to
page 48) are to be traced on
other paper to make the
"paper sculptures".

▶6

この頁の型紙を、薄手の白ケント
紙に現寸もしくは拡大トレースを
し、作業を始めます。まずアーチ
状になる部分、型紙中央部にある
直線の切り込み線にしたがい帯を
作ります。次に両端の直方体とな
る部分を作ります。折れ線に定規
をあて折ると、きれいに折れます。
最後にのりしろに接着剤をつけ固
定します。

◀6

Trace the pattern on thin
white paper in the same size
or enlarging it. For the arch
section cut in strips along the
lines in the middle. Next,
make two pillars at both ends.
If you place a ruler on the
folding line, you can fold it
very neatly. Lastly, glue them
together as indicated on the
pattern.

▶7

実物は銀の厚手のボードに切り込
みを入れ、その切り込みに赤、青、
黄、緑、銀の細い帯にねじりを加
え、差し込んだものです。作り方
は、厚手のボードと各色の細い帯
で簡単にできます。帯の交錯と銀
にうつり込んだ影の面白さが、こ
の作品のポイントです。

◀7

Long strips of paper colored in
red, blue, yellow, green, and
silver are twined and planted
in small cuts made on silver
board. The mingled effect of
reflections, shadows, colors,
and lines is remarkable.

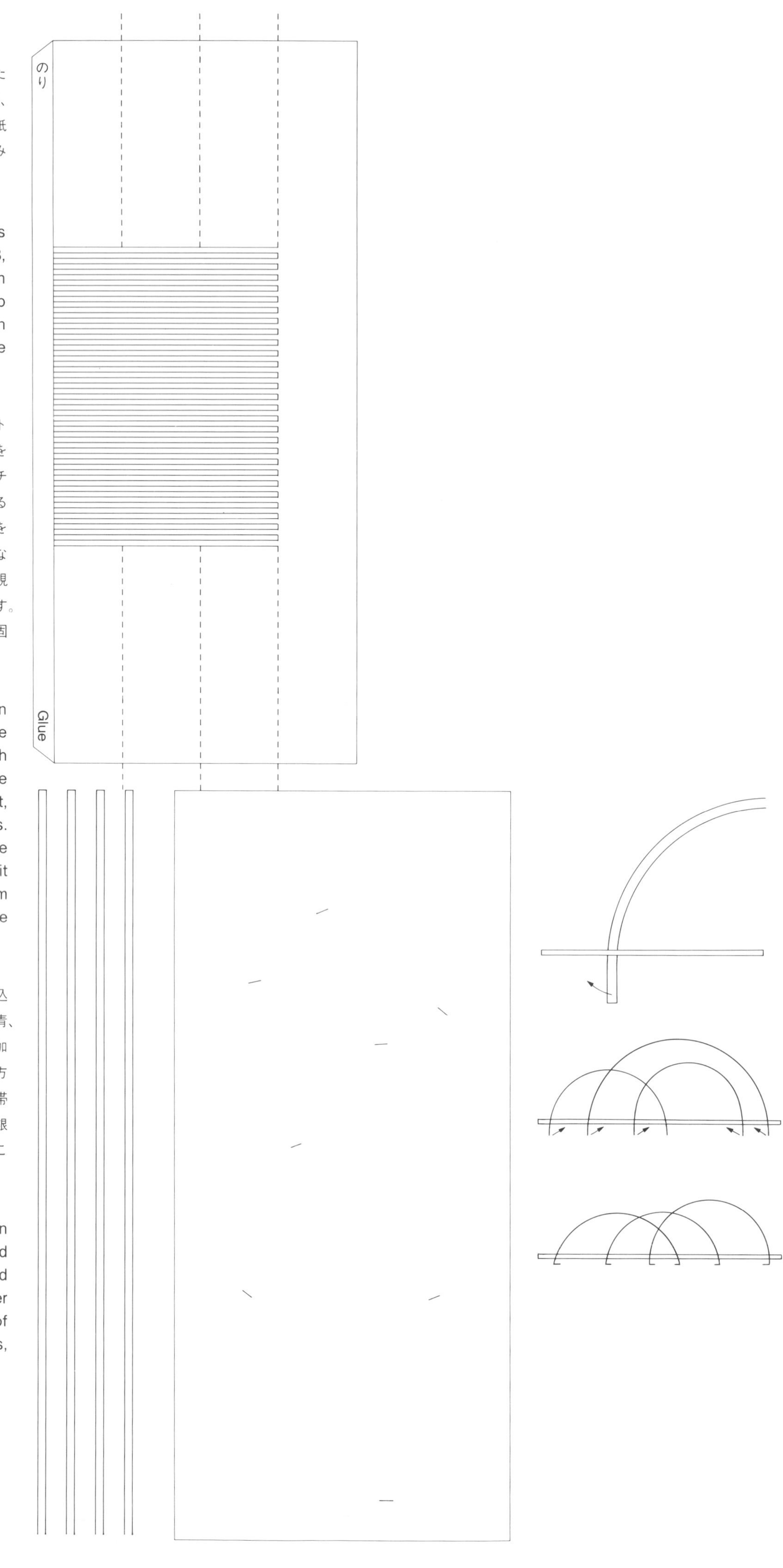

2種類のやや厚手の淡い色調を持つグラデーションペーパーを貼り合わせ、型紙を鉛筆できれいにトレースします。帯の中央にある円は、カッター付きコンパスで2点を残し慎重に切り離し、折れ線に沿って折り曲げます。最後に円の角度を傾け、色の変化を出します。

◖11

Glue two sheets of different colored gradation paper to each other and make them into one sheet. Preferably, the paper to be on the thicker side and the colors to be of soft shade. Now trace the pattern on this paper neatly with a pencil. Then, cut a row of circles as indicated with a circle cutter leaving two points each for a circle uncut which serve as joints. After folding the paper along the lines, arrange the angles of circles so as to get good color effect.

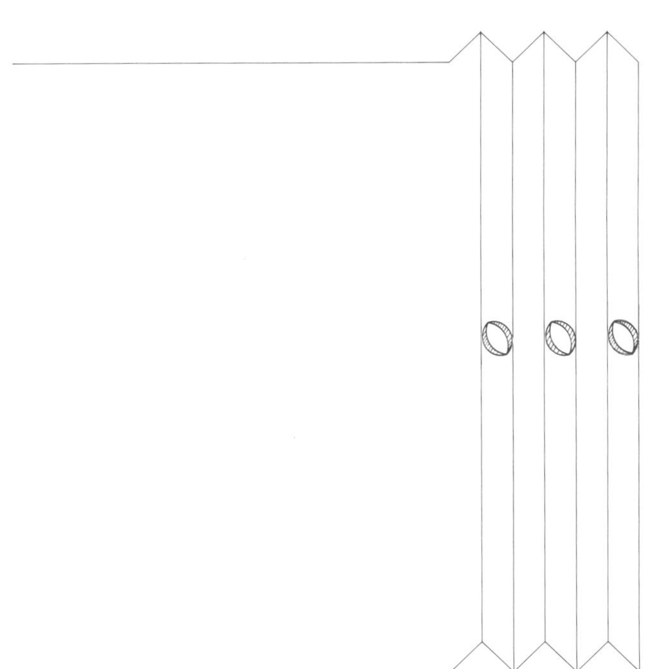

◗13

星を擬人化した作品です。やや厚目の紙にトレースし帯状にした紙の端の星型を先の細いカッターで切り、中央の切り取り線に沿ってカッターを入れます。飾る時は脚の部分を前後に開き、美しい曲線を作るだけです。

◖13

Maybe a starman?
Trace the pattern on thicker paper so that it can stand on its two legs. First, cut a star with a mat knife out of the strip, then cut along the center line indicated on the pattern. When you display, open these two legs, one to the front, one to the back.

表面に光沢のある白いやや厚手の
紙にトレースしてください。星型
を先の細いカッターで切り抜き、
次に帯状のゆるやかなカーブを切
り抜きます。飾る時は長方形の方
に残った半円に角度をつけると、
微妙な光と影を演出できます。

17

Trace the pattern on glossy
white thick paper. Cut a star
first with a pointed mat knife,
then cut that gently curved
strip out. The same way with
the other two. When you display, arrange the angles of the
curve strips in harmony with
the curves left on the screen.
You will get a delicate effect
of light and shadow.

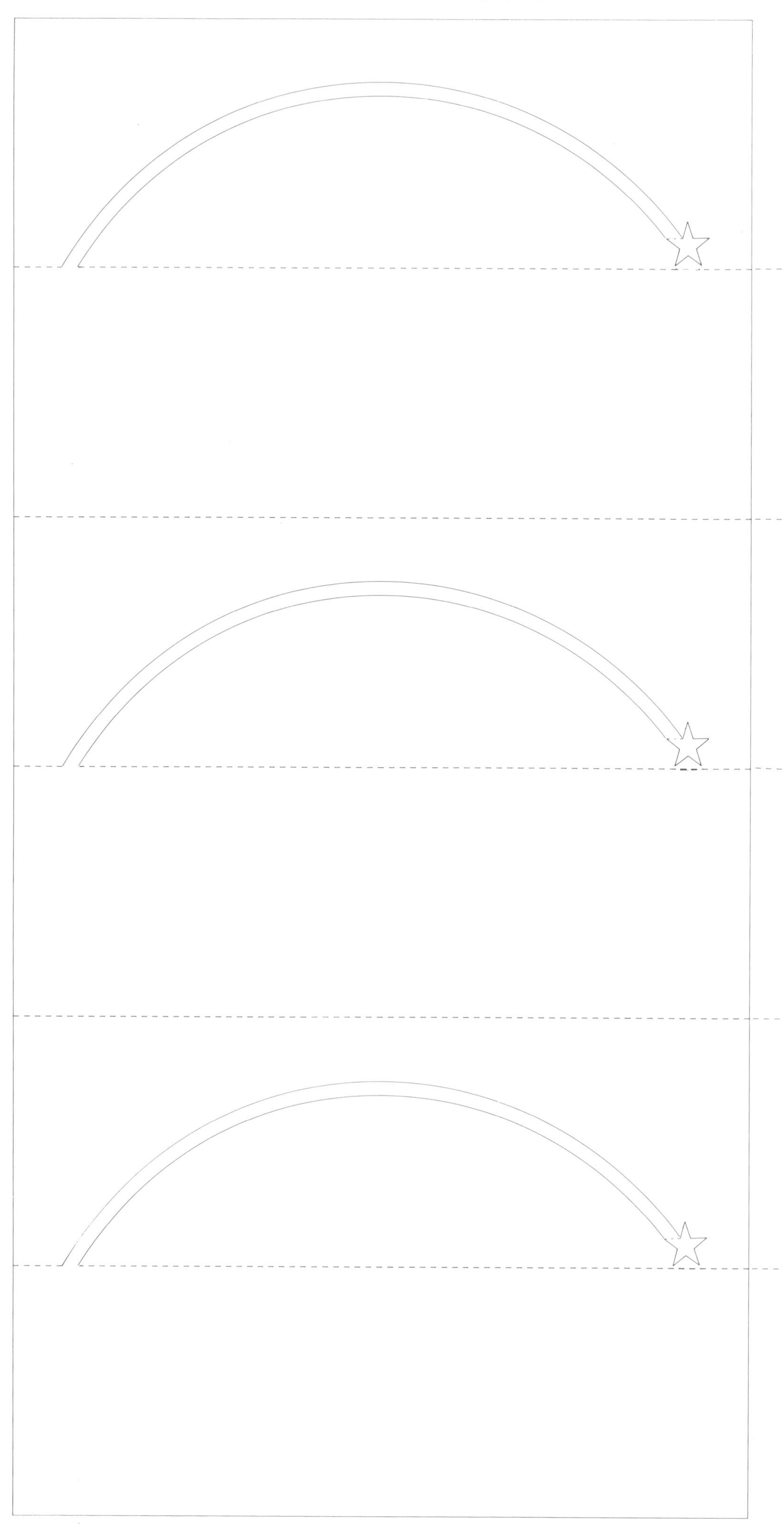

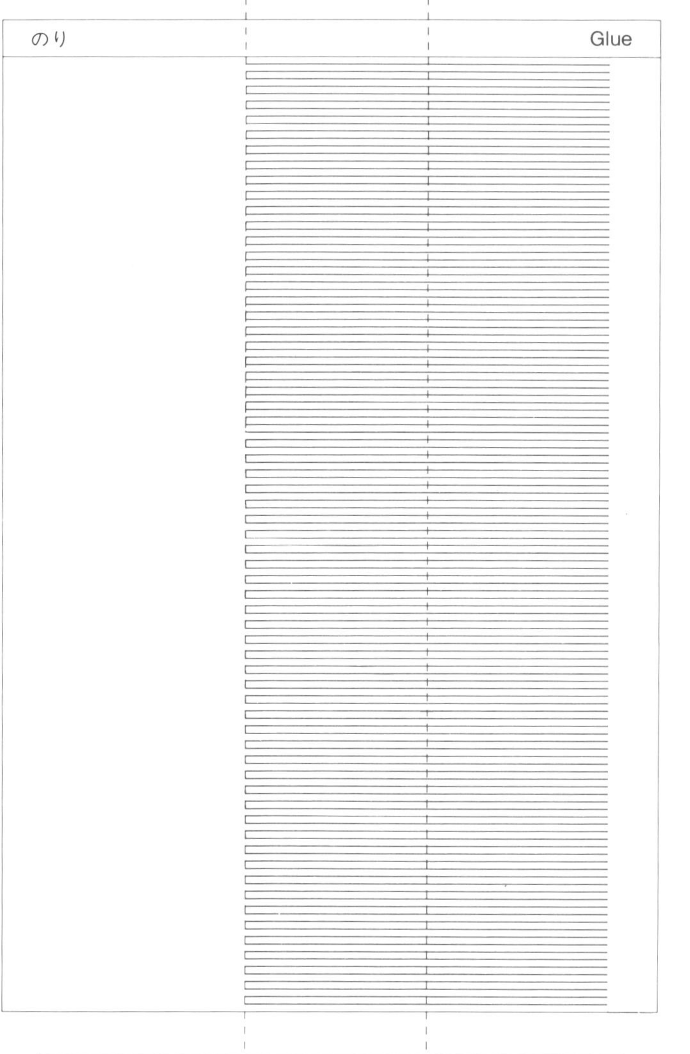

▶18

表面が赤く裏面が白い薄手の色紙の裏面にトレースします。作り方は、まず定規を使いカッターで細い帯を作ります。次に細い帯の上端を内側に折り曲げ、細い帯の中央部にも軽く折れ線を入れておきます。最後に円筒状にし、上から軽く押して形を整えると完成です。

◀18

Trace the pattern on thin (not too thin) paper, one side red one side white. Using a ruler and a mat knife, cut along the lines into narrow strips. Then fold the upper side of strips (rectangular part) inward (to the red side) and also make a light fold (on the red side) at the center of the strips. Lastly, make a cylinder of it and press the top down into the shape you want.

▶19

作り方は作品18と似ています。真っ白な紙に型紙をトレースし、定規とカッターで細い帯を作り円筒にし、さらに両端を接着し円形にするだけです。

表紙の作品はこの作品19のバリエーションで、円形ではなくメビウスの帯のようにねじって両端を接着したものです。

◀19

The way of making this work is similar to the way of making Piece 18. Trace the pattern on white paper, cut into narrow strips with a ruler and a mat knife and make a cylinder of it. Then glue both ends together into the shape of a doughnut.

The work on the cover is a variation of this work. Not of doughnut shape, but twisted once like a mobius' band and glued at the both ends.

2つの作品がありますが、どちら
も同じ考え方、円と三角形、長方
形を基本に作ったモビールで、組
み合わせと配色がポイントです。
型紙を2種類の色紙と厚手の紙に
トレースし、カッターなどで切り
抜き、厚手の紙の表裏に色紙を貼
りつけるだけです。

You see two mobiles here, but
the ideas are the same. The
combination of shapes and
colors is very important in
these works.
Trace the pattern on two
kinds of colored paper and a
sheet of thicker paper.
Sandwich the thicker one
between two colored ones
and glue.

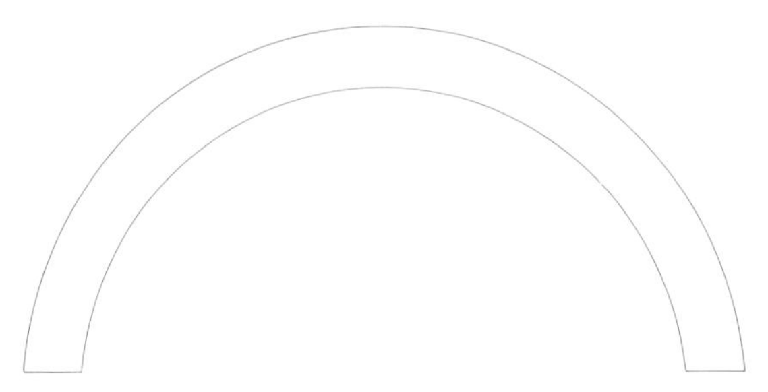

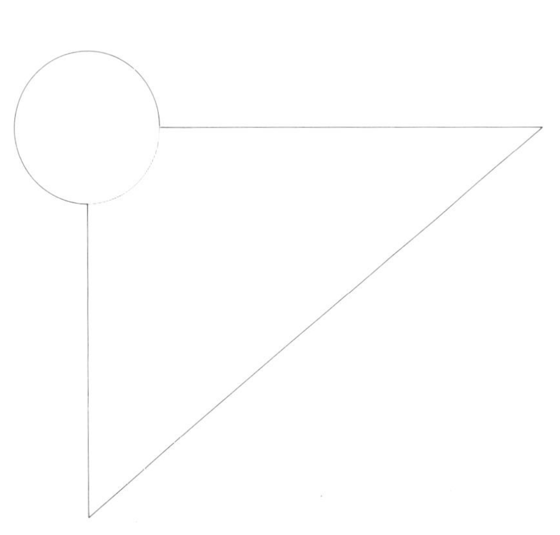

不規則な動きと微妙な色の変化を
楽しむことができるモビールです。
やや厚手の表面に色のついた紙に、
４つの大きさの異なる円をトレー
スします。トレースした各円に切
り込みを入れ、その切り込みを入
れた部分を重ねあわせると円錐が
できます。これを糸で４つつなげ
ると完成です。

◀25

In this mobile you can enjoy
irregular movements of forms
and delicate changing of
color. Trace four circles of
different sizes on fairly thick
paper with one side colored.
After cutting out four circles,
cut each one along the line
from its edge to the center.
Glueing the edges together,
you can make four shallow
cones. Now, hang these four
one by one on a piece of
thread.

厚手の銀紙に、３つのドーナツ状
の円をトレースし、カッター付き
のコンパスで切り抜きます。この
作品はこれまでの考え方とは異な
り、枝に２本の糸で「かみ彫刻」
をぶらさげています。風で微妙に
揺れ、美しい軌跡を作ります。

Trace three doughnut-shaped
circles on thick silver paper
and cut them out with a circle
cutter. This work is unique in
its way, as three circles are
hung on two pieces of thread
from a branch of a tree. A
slight breeze gives to the work
delicate movements.

この頁以降の型紙は、「かみ彫刻」
を実際に作るためのものです。収
載した作品は 1、2、3、4、5、8、
9、10、12、14、15、16、21、22、
23、24の16点です。

Pattern 2

The patterns from this page
on are for making the actual
"paper sculptures".   The
works are Piece Nos. 1, 2, 3, 4,
5, 8, 9, 10, 12, 14, 15, 16, 21, 22,
23 and 24.

▶1

リフレクション（反射）を楽しむこ
とができる作品です。まず型紙の
下の正方形の裏側に赤い紙を貼り、
切り込み線の描かれている方から
五角形となる部分の各三角形の底
辺部分を残し、カッターで切り離
し外側に折り曲げます。裏側に来
る正方形の方は、太陽を連想させ
るパターンを切り抜き、全体を箱
状に折ります。

◀1

This is the work in which you
can enjoy the reflections of
light.
First, glue red colored paper to
the back of the lower square
of the pattern. Cut five inside
lines of the pentagon, leaving
outside lines uncut. Fold the
five triangle flaps outward.
Now, on the upper square, cut
the sun-shaped design with a
mat knife. Then fold the whole
thing into a flat box and glue.

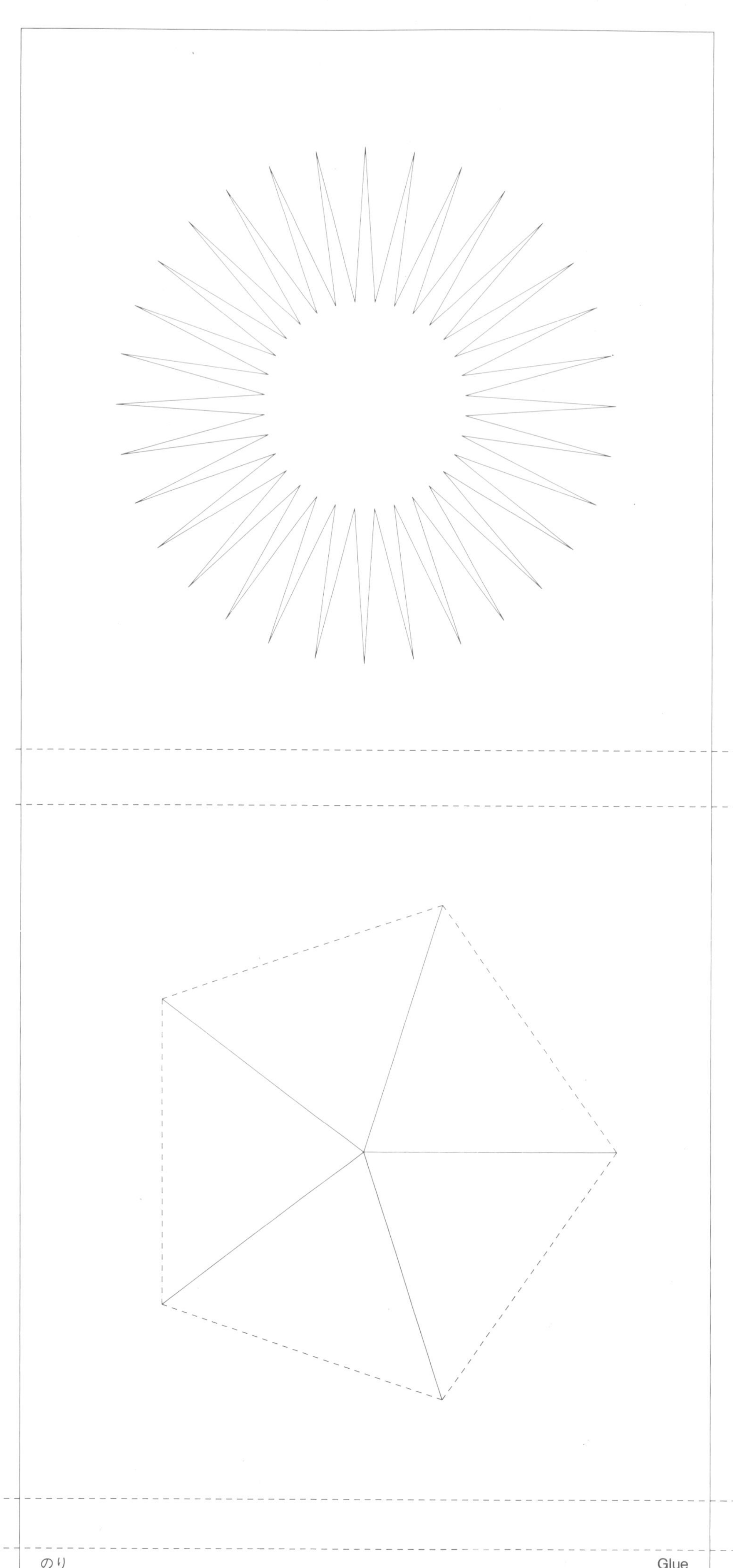

のり   Glue

●2

作品Iと同様に「かみ彫刻」の裏
側に色紙を貼り、光の変化による
リフレクションを楽しむ作品です。
作り方は、型紙の下端の長方形の
裏側に赤い紙を貼り、太陽となる
部分をカッターで切り抜きます。
最後に両面テープなどの接着剤を
使い、三角柱を作ると完成です。

◀2

As in Piece I, you can also
enjoy the reflections of light in
this work. To make this piece,
glue red paper to the back of
the rectangle you see at the
lower part of the pattern, then
cut the sun-ray design out
with a mat knife. Using two-
sided adhesive tape, glue
together.

月とも丸窓とも見える円とすすき
を組み合わせた「かみ彫刻」です。
型紙に沿ってカッターで切り、ま
ず長方形を作ります。そして正面
にくる正方形の中央にカッター付
きコンパスで円を作り、もう一つ
の正方形にすすきの模様をカッタ
ーで作ります。すすきの位置は、
中央より下の部分に入れるのがポ
イントです。

This work suggests full moon
or maybe a round window and
susuki (Japanese pampas
grass). Cut the rectangle with
a mat knife along the lines
indicated on the pattern and
fold it in half. Now, you have
two flaps of a square. Cut a
circle out of one with a circle
cutter, and cut blades of grass
out of the other with a pointed
mat knife.

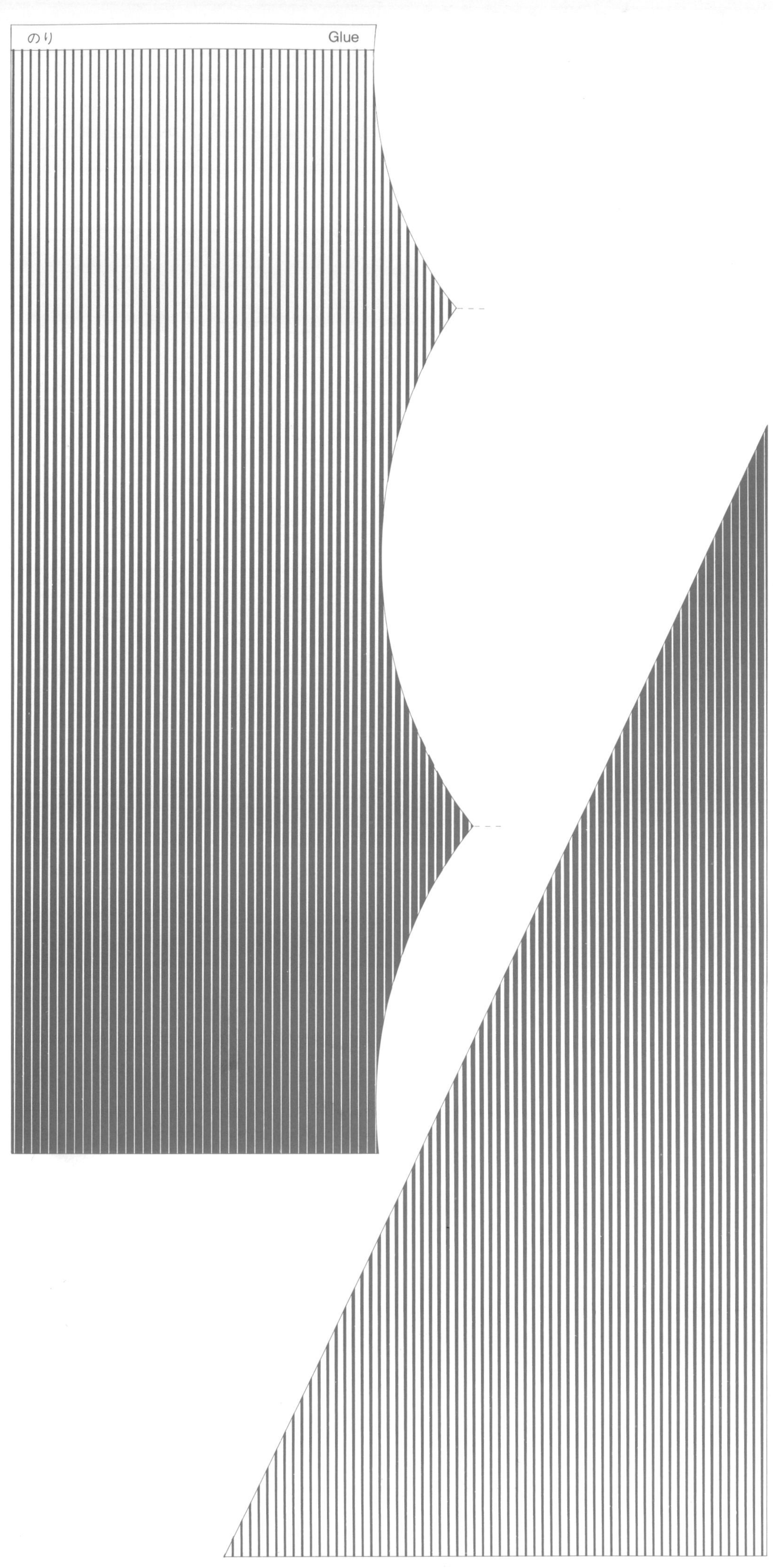

▶4

2つの部分からなる、線と形の美
しさを楽しむ「かみ彫刻」です。
上に来る三角形の部分は型紙を切
り抜き、印刷された面が表になる
ようにします。下の部分は上に来
るカーブがポイントですから、切
り取り線に沿ってカッターで慎重
に切り、楕円状の円筒にするだけ
です。

◀4

This "paper sculpture" con-
sisting of two forms has very
pleasing lines and shapes.
First, cut carefully one form
out of the lower part of the
pattern and make an oval
cylinder. Then place the triangle in it so that the printed
side can be seen from the
front.

型紙と同じ大きさの長方形を 4 つ
作り、その裏面に赤、黄、青、緑
の光沢のある色紙を貼りつけます。
接着剤が乾燥したら、切り取り線
が明示されている表面からパンチ
で穴を開けます。円と円を結ぶ直
線部分は、先の細いカッターで帯
状に切り抜き作ります。最後に中
央より折り曲げると完成です。

◀5

Make four rectangular sheets
of paper of the same size as
indicated on the pattern and
glue glossy colored paper of
red, yellow, blue, and green to
the back of each. Punch holes
as shown on the pattern.
Straight lines between re-
spective holes are cut in strips
by a mat knife.   Then fold
each sheet at the center.

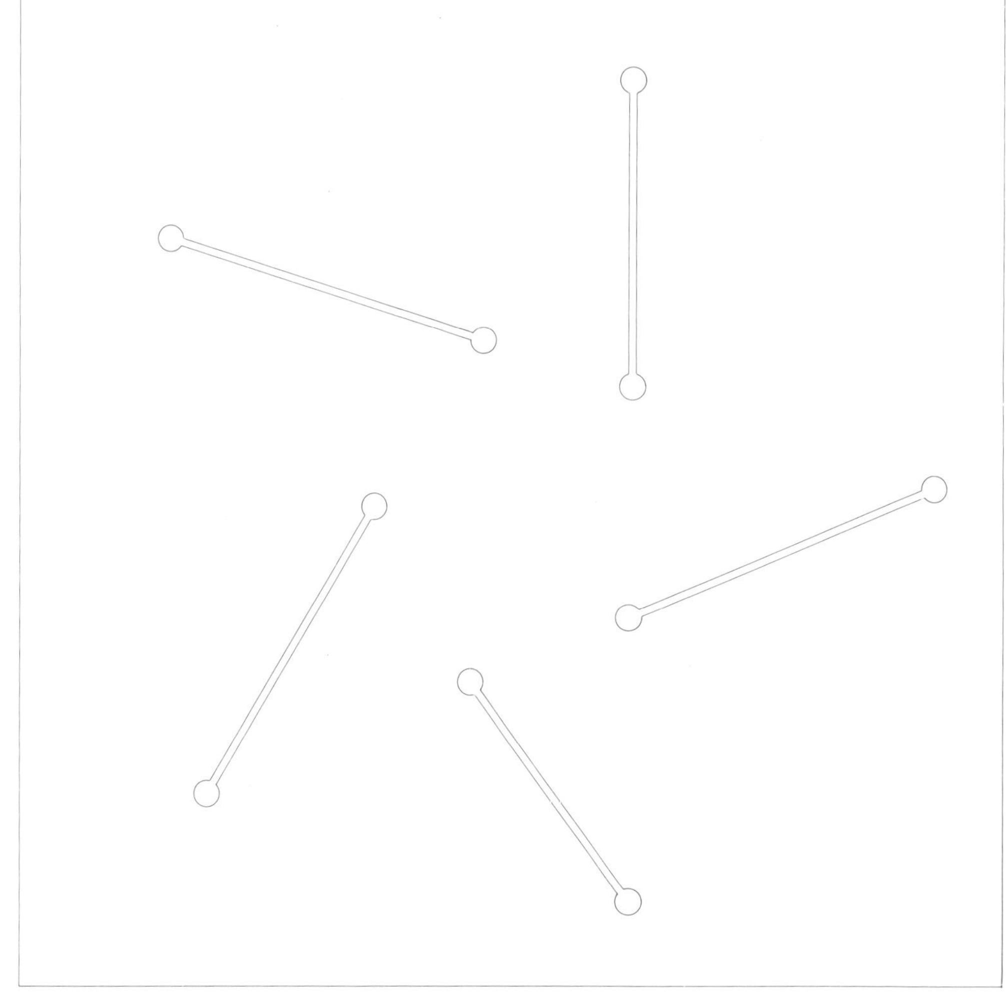

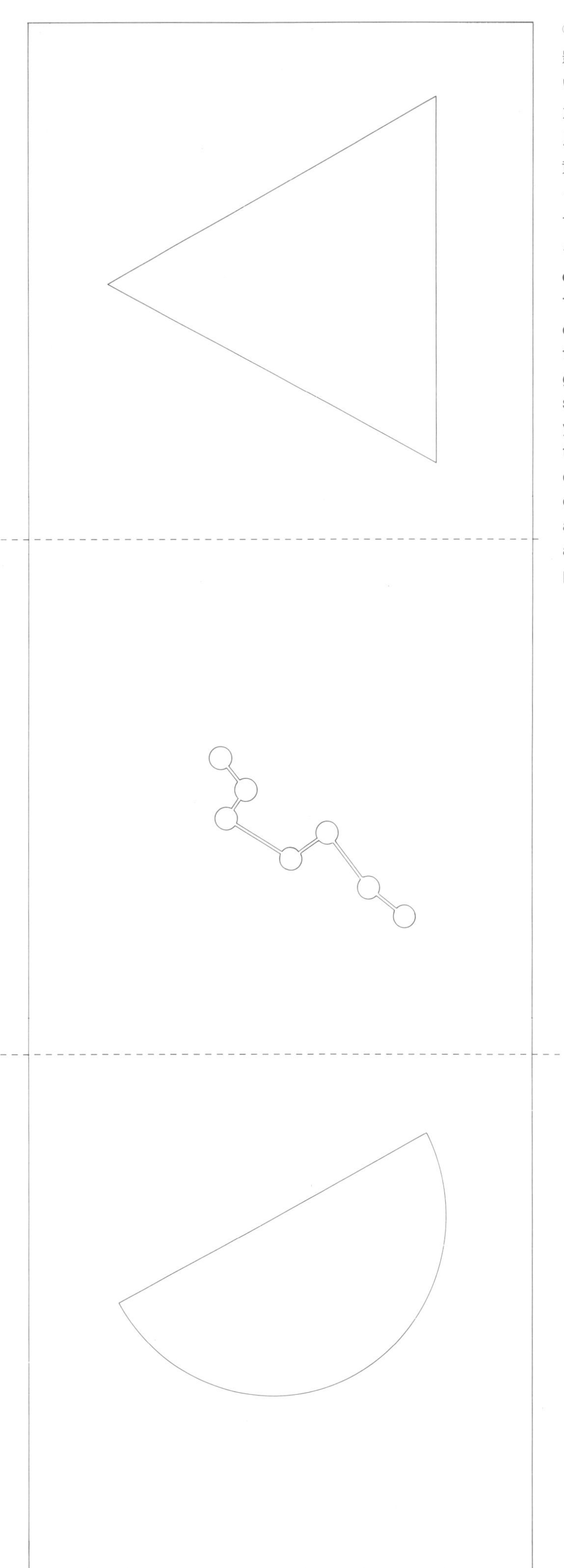

影と色彩のリフレクションが楽しい作品です。山をイメージした三角形の裏面には淡い緑の色紙を、月をイメージした半円の裏面には黄色の色紙を貼り、カッターとカッター付きコンパスで切り抜きます。中央に来る星は、パンチで穴を開けカッターで直線を作ります。

◀8

This is a work in which you can enjoy shadows and reflections of colors. Glue pale green paper to the back of the square with the triangle, and yellow paper to the back of the square with the semicircle. Using a mat knife and a circle cutter, cut the triangle and semicircle out. The stars and the lines are cut with a paper punch and a mat knife.

星型と月をイメージした曲線で構
成された「かみ彫刻」です。作り
方は簡単です。型紙に沿って慎重
に星型を切り抜きます。大きなカ
ーブはカッター付きコンパスで、
小さな円はカッターで切り、ハサ
ミで整えます。線の美しさがこの
「かみ彫刻」の生命ですから、カ
ットは慎重に行ないます。

Cut the star with a mat knife.
Cut the bigger curves with a
circle cutter, and the small
circle with a mat knife and
scissors. In this paper sculpture the neatness of the lines
is very important, therefore,
cutting should be done with
the utmost care.

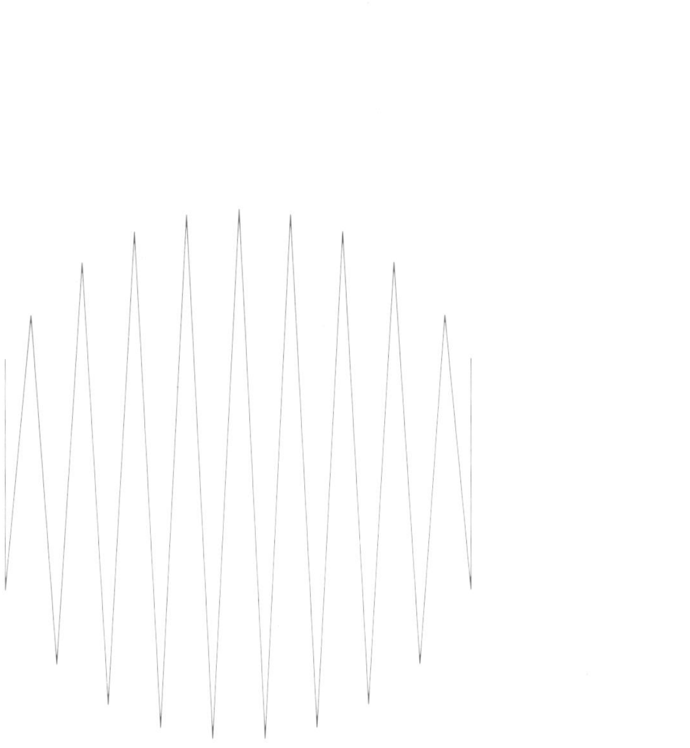

◗**10**

上から見ると半円形に見える「かみ彫刻」です。面積の大きい長方形の中央にある矢印状の模様を、定規を使いカッターで切り込みを入れます。面積の小さい長方形を裏に来るように折り、面積の大きい長方形を半円形にすると矢印状の模様が飛び出してきます。

◖**10**

When you look down this work from above, it looks like a semicircle. Using a ruler and a mat knife, cut the arrow-like design printed on the larger rectangle of the pattern. Then fold the smaller rectangle toward the back of the bigger one. After that, bend the bigger one sidewise into a semicircle. As you do that, the arrow-like design protrudes automatically.

●12

３つの三角形と円弧で作られた美
しいフォルムを持つ「かみ彫刻」
です。型紙の指示通り３つの三角
形を作り、折って三角錐にします。
円弧はカッターかカッター付きの
コンパスで切り抜きます。この円
弧は湿気によりカーブの角度が変
わるので、注意してください。

◐12

A beautiful harmony of three
triangles and a long arch with
a tiny circle at its end. As
indicated on the pattern,
make a pyramid of three triangles. A mat knife or a circle
cutter can be used to cut the
arch part. Pay special atten-
tion to the arch as the angle of
its curve might be changed by
moisture.

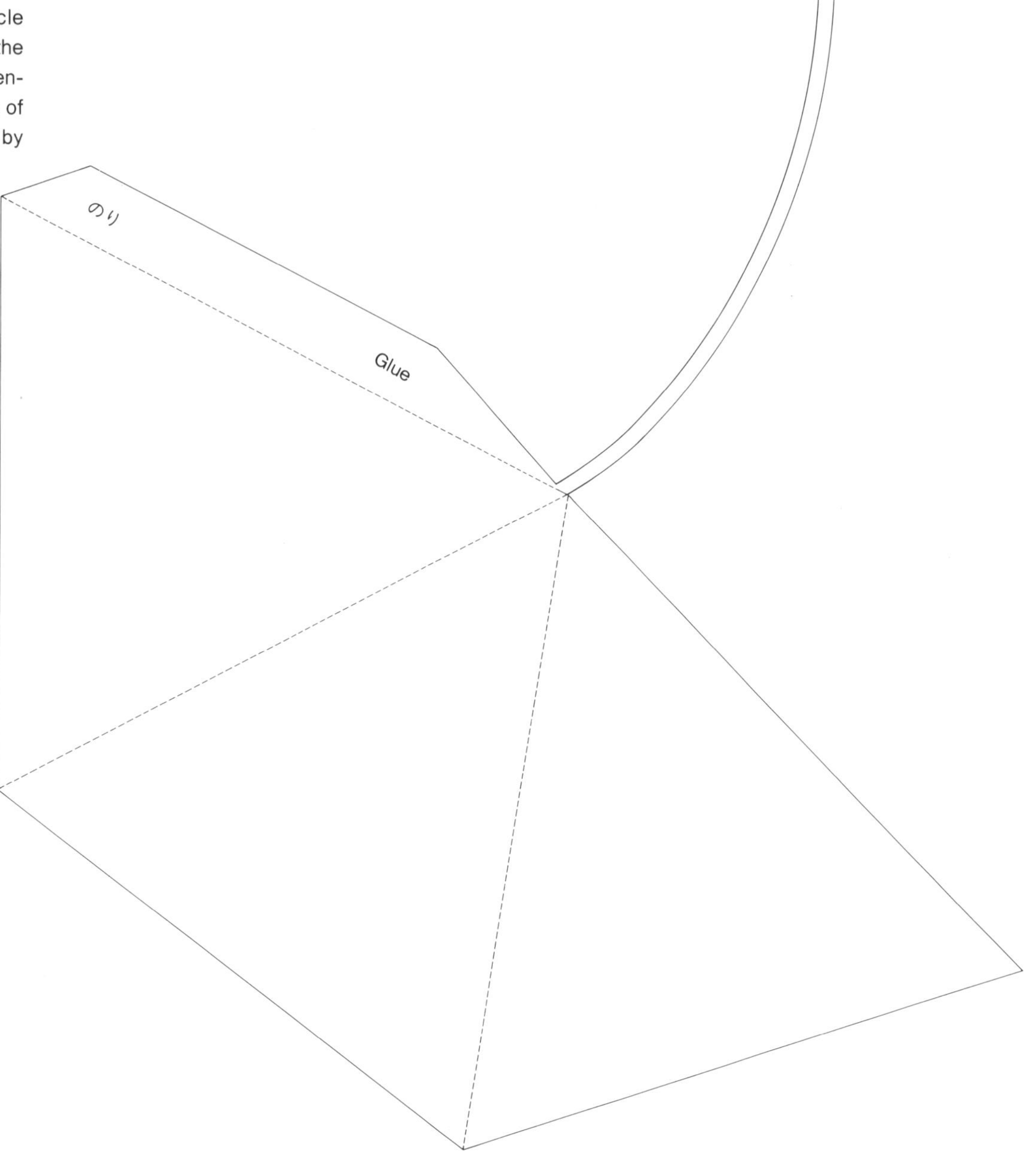
のり
Glue

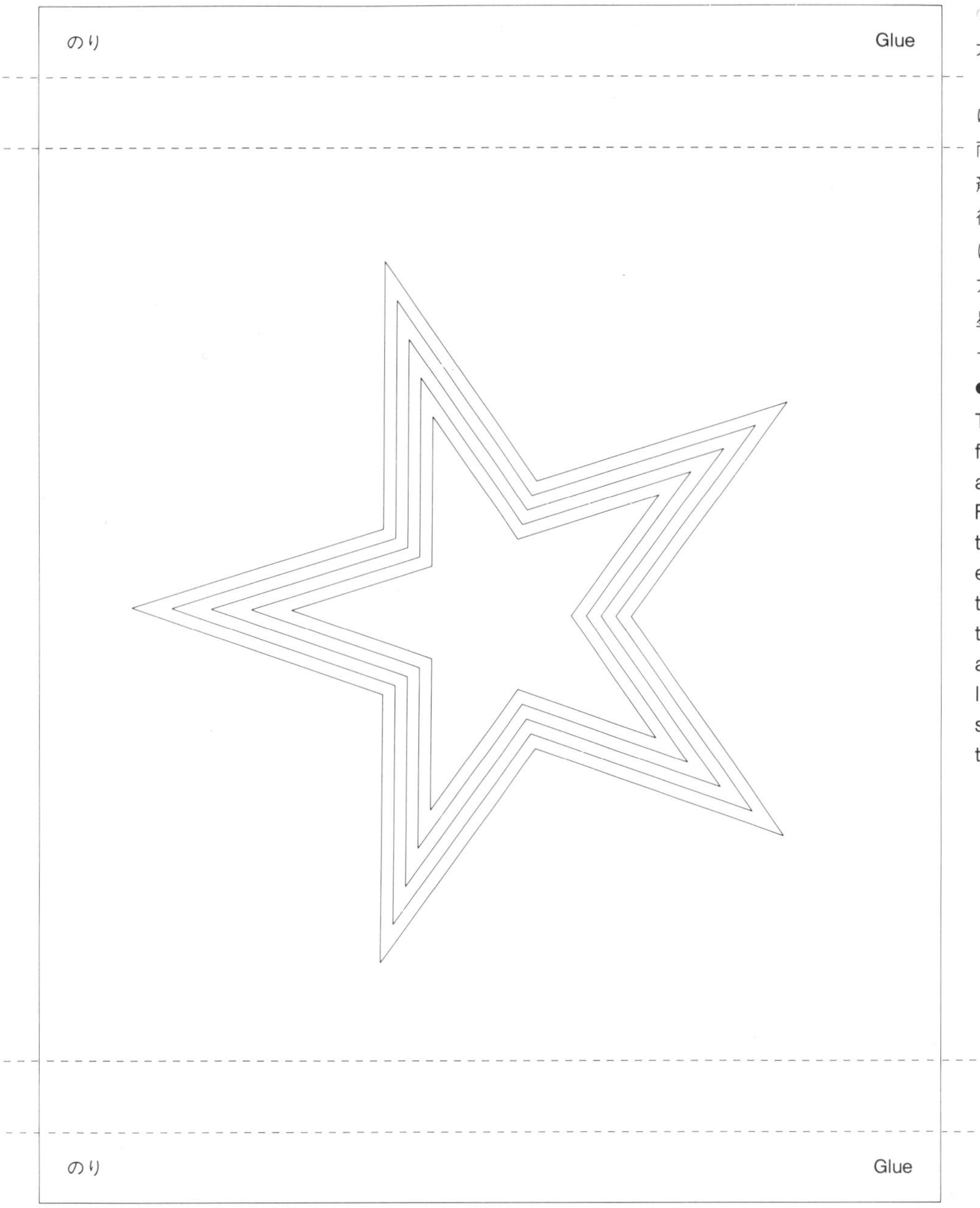

▶14

大きさの異なる星型を持つ型紙を、5つ重ね合わせたものです。型紙に描かれた星型を丹念に切り抜き、両端を折り曲げ、のりしろに接着剤をつけて貼り合わせます。一番、後に来る型紙は星型を切り抜くだけです。残りの4つの型紙の作り方は、外形はこの型紙をトレース、星型は内側にある4本の線をトレースして作ります。

◁14

This work is simply a layer of five sheets of paper each with a star, but of different size. First, cut a star carefully out of the pattern and fold the both ends as indicated. To make the other four sheets, trace the pattern on other paper, and as for stars, trace the four lines drawn inside the biggest star. Lastly glue all five of them togerther.

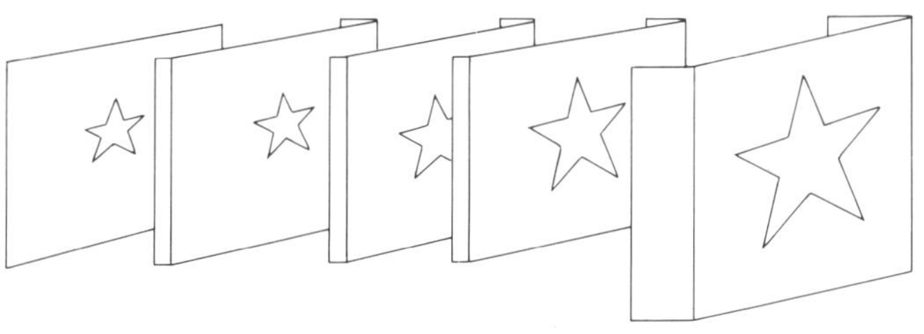

一枚の紙に宇宙全体を表現、最後
に金粉をまいたものです。太陽は
カッターで、月はカッター付きコ
ンパスで、楕円は先の細いカッタ
ーで慎重に2点を残し切り抜きま
す。切り抜いた楕円は、美しく見
える角度に調節します。

Heavenly bodies and golden
stardust on a sheet of paper.
Cut the sun with a mat knife,
the moon with a circle cutter,
and the ellipse with a pointed
mat knife very carefully leaving two points uncut as joints.
The piece inside the ellipse is
moveable,so it may be altered
for different effects.

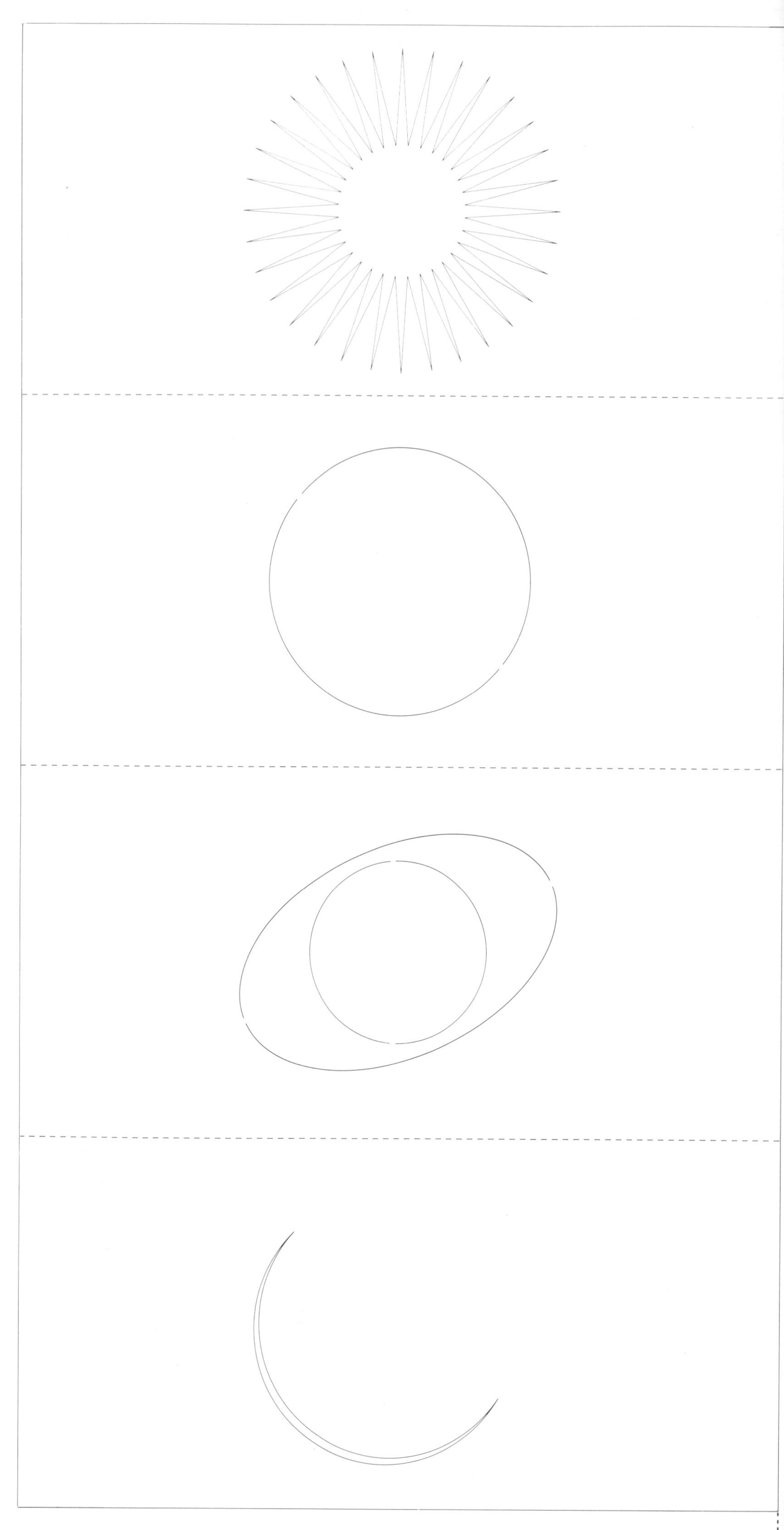

●16

星型と円で構成された、宇宙船にも見える「かみ彫刻」です。型紙の指示通り、カッター付きコンパスで円を切り抜きます。細い帯状の部分は、先に星型をカッターで切り抜き、その後に帯の部分を切り抜く方が作業はスムースにいきます。

◖16

A star and a circular object. This might remind you of a space ship. Cut the circle with a circle cutter. Then cut the strip. But before doing that, cut the star first. It is much easier that way.

●21
シンプルな外形と、中央の紡錘形
を切り抜き、その上に同じ形をし
た淡い色のグラデーションペーパ
ーを貼り、回転するように糸で吊
るします。

◐21
In this mobile, you will enjoy
its simple shape and the
changing of the color of the
spindle-shaped object. Cut
the spindle out and glue gradation paper of the same
shape to it. Then hang the
whole thing on a piece of
thread in such a way that the
spindle may spin,too.

作品21よりも作り方は複雑です。まず型紙を指示通り正方形に切り抜き、パンチで穴を開けます。次に穴と穴を結ぶ直線と曲線をカッターで切り抜きます。最後に中央の曲線部を切り抜き、グラデーションペーパーを表裏に貼った、帯をはさみこみます。はさみ込む帯は型紙にはありませんので、１cm幅のものを別に作ってください。

◖22

This is more complicated than Piece 21 is. First, cut the square out of the pattern and make holes on it with a paper punch. Next, cut straight lines and a curved line between holes as indicated. Lastly, cut out a curved line in the middle and put a long strip of paper in this cut. This strip is not printed on the pattern, therefore, make it yourself, the width is 1 cm. Glue the gradation paper to both sides.

内側に貼ってあるグリーンとピンク
クの色が、角度により微妙に変化
するモビールです。型紙の指示に
従い、表裏となる正方形の中に細
い帯を作り、その裏側にグリーン
とピンクの帯を貼り、最後に箱状
にします。この細い帯の干渉によ
り、グリーンやピンクの面積が変
化し、色の濃淡がでるわけです。

Through the slits of this flat
box, you can see the delicate
changing of pink and green
colors.　As indicated make
narrow slits on two squares
and glue pink and green strips
to the whole thing. Then, hang
it on a piece of thread.

▶24
パターンを印刷された型紙を切り、中央から折り曲げ貼り合わせます。上端に来る円はカッター付きコンパスで切り抜きます。最後にアクセントとなる黄や赤の色紙を好きな形に切り、P.34−35の写真のように取り付け、糸で吊すとモビールが完成します。

◀24
Cut out pattern as indicated. Fold it at the middle and glue back to back. Cut the circle out from the upper part of it with a circle cutter. Lastly, cut red or yellow paper into any shape and glue to the lower part of it as shown in P34-35. This gives the piece accent.